Helping A Sister

*5 Critical Components for Creating
Global Communities of Change*

Maxine L. Johnson

ISBN-13: 978-0578425337

Legal Disclaimer
While none of the stories in this book are fabricated, some of the names and details may have been changed to protect the privacy of the individuals mentioned. Although the author and publisher have made every effort to ensure that the information in this book was correct at press time, the author and publisher do not assume and hereby disclaim any liability to any party for any loss, damage, or disruption caused by errors or omissions, whether such errors or omissions result from negligence, accident, or any other cause.

Ordering Information
Helping A Sister may be purchased in large quantities at a discount for educational, business, or sales promotional use. For information, email: www.helpingasisterministry@gmail.com.

Visit www.helpingasisterinternational.com to partner with our movement!

Dedication

This book is dedicated to my mother, Sandra McMillian; and to my grandmothers, Helen Waller and Stella McMillan, who were both affectionately known as "Sister."

I dedicate this book to every sister, friend, and mentor who helped me along the way, and to, Reverend Glenn and Deborah Shepherd--thank you for planting!

As iron sharpens iron, so one sister sharpens another.
Proverbs 27:17

Contents

Introduction

I celebrate her because she is a queen.

We are different in many ways, but in other ways we are the same. It has taken me years to get here because I did not understand her or know her, but now, even with her idiosyncrasies, I celebrate her because she is my sister. Our struggles may be different, but we are similar in so many ways. She is not perfect. Still, she is a queen.

She is my sister.

Why can't I help a sister?

Why can't I help a sister to realize she doesn't have to share that man? Why can't I help a sister by telling her not to escape her pain by using alcohol or drugs. Why can't I help a sister and tell her that she doesn't have to buy her children's love because their father cheated on her? Why can't I? Why don't I? I don't because she is who I was. She is who I feared I could become. When I see her it is as if a mirror is turned back onto me and I am forced to examine myself. So often I do not like what I see. I am hard on her. I am harder on myself. Then I realize that before I can help a sister, I have to embrace that I am a queen too and that in order for me to truly help a sister, I have to help myself first.

Sometimes, I see my sister and I think, "Why can't that be me?" That sister has it going on. I congratulate her in my mind, but I am really thinking, "Why can't that be me?" I want more, but I am not sure how to get it. I think again to myself, "If I ask for help, she will look down on me. Perhaps she will think I am her flunky or that I am just some gofer who she can have do things she does not want to do?" I admire her, but my pride won't let me tell my sister.

Forget about asking if she can mentor or help me, my mind races again, "Ah, I will do it on my own. Google will tell you everything." Yes, Google can tell you some things, but it does not tell you how to navigate the emotional issues you go through when you feel rejected. So, I am where I began – wishing that I were that sister and having no clue how to evolve from who I am into who I wished I were.

It has been said that, "Comfort and growth cannot coexist." This explains why we so often feel that we have to do more and more. It also gives us insight into the fact that in order to grow we have to move, and it follows that once you decide to move, especially in directions that you have never moved before, you have to ask for help so that you can achieve what you desire to achieve. At times we do not move forward because of pride. At times we do not move forward because we do not want to lose friends, but sacrifice is necessary for growth. Giving up people, places and things to help a sister out is a requirement on one's journey to success.

On my personal journey, I remember struggling to answer important questions such as: Who am I? What do I want? What do I like? What do I dislike? Where do I see myself in the future? Too often the sad truth was that I did not know.

I wanted to help others and I wanted to do more, but I had no clue about how to do that because I did not know myself. I was not clear enough then to know where I was going. I'd be the blind leading the blind and that was not my goal at all. So, I had to learn to, as they tell you when preparing to fly, put the mask on myself before I could place the mask on my sister. I had to realize that if I was no good, I could not help someone else. My journey truly began when I took the courage and the time to discover everything that I could about a certain sister--that sister is me.

I made the time and investments necessary to grow, gain clarity and heal, and in 2011 God placed the vision and gift of *Helping a Sister* into my heart.

Through my work with women both domestically and internationally, I developed the *5 Critical Components for Creating Global Communities of Change.* When implemented by women, like you and like me, who are committed and daring enough to listen and to love one another through good times and bad, these five components of H.A.S will contribute significantly to changing the world one sister at a time. The 5 components of H.A.S., when properly executed, lead to transformation in the lives of people and communities. They are:

1. See

2. Share

3. Care

4. Change

5. Create

In H.A.S., I share my stories of triumph and many of my trials too. My hope and prayer are that my transparency and my sharing of the lessons I learned, will encourage and equip you to become a partner in healing hurting women everywhere, thereby growing the H.A.S. movement both in America and abroad.

Together, let's explore how these five critical components work in ways that lead to helping sisters everywhere.

Maxine

SEE

Chapter 1

I See You and You are Not Alone

"Remove your mask. Receive your sister's love."

~Maxine L. Johnson

Trust and vulnerability are two essential elements that, when present, add value and depth to any relationship. True sisterhood is no different. We give so much of ourselves as women, wives, mothers, sisters, professionals and friends, that despite being in the company of a variety of people every day, we can feel invisible.

I have had the blessing of working with and ministering to women from a variety of backgrounds and socioeconomic statuses for many years. These women ranged from very accomplished professionals, to amazing stay-at-home mothers, to savvy business owners, to women in crisis, and often any one woman could be a combination of them all. Interestingly, all the women had something in common -- at some phase of their journey, they all needed to know that their effort and hard work (even when they were not at their bests) was seen, and that they were not alone.

We have all felt invisible or abandoned, but isn't it interesting that those are not the stories we tell, if we tell those stories at all? Helping a sister requires you to tell your story. Another sister needs to be seen by you. Another sister needs to hear from you.

I Have Been Where you Are

I remember an instance in my life when this was especially true. An announcement was made at church that a member's father had passed away. He was found dead in his home. She was a young woman. My father died when I was young too.

I felt her pain.

Around the time of that young woman's father's death, she and I happened to both attend the same service at my church.

After the service, what felt to me like throngs of people, were walking up to her, hugging her, praying with her, and sharing encouraging words with her. I looked from a distance, but I did not join the crowd.

I had an impression on my heart and heard the Holy Spirit say to me, "Go. Tell her that you were once there. Let her know that you lost your dad the same way." Now I will be honest. I was thinking, "What? Lord, I am here. I am standing right here. Way over here, God. I am minding my business. Look, do you see what I see? She is surrounded by people. She is overwhelmed with love and hugs, prayers, and words of encouragement and comfort from basically the entire church. I'm good right here, God. She doesn't need to hear from me too." I continued to plead my case, "Besides, God, I don't even really know her like that."

Nonetheless, with all my resistance and all my excuses as to why she did not need to hear from me, the press upon my heart to go and speak with that young, grieving woman would not leave me.

So, I finally went up to her, looked her in the eye and said, "I've been where you are."

Daddy's Girl

It was 1995 and my brother called me to tell me that my dad wouldn't wake up. I immediately told my husband (at that time) that I had to go to my dad's house because my dad wasn't waking up. My husband told me to go and said he would be right behind me. When I arrived at my dad's house, there he was, lying in the bed with one hand under his head. On the side of the bed was a forty ounce -- a big bottle of beer. Daddy looked like he was just asleep, so I touched him, but his body was cold and when I looked more closely, I noticed that his lips were blue.

It was surreal.

My daddy was dead.

"But he couldn't be dead," I reasoned. "He couldn't be dead because he just told me the other day that he had purchased toys for my sons. The toys were in the closet. So, he couldn't be dead. I mean, he said that he was going to pick up my oldest son from school in the fall since he'd just retired." The reasons he could not be dead continued to swirl through my head like a professional racecar around the track

"No! My Daddy could not be dead!"

I was daddy's girl. Even through all of his drunken moments, to be sure that he would not hurt himself, I'd take on the role of mother to make sure that my daddy did not hurt himself. "No, he isn't dead." The mantra boomed incessant and loud like a drum in my head. "He isn't dead." I sat on the edge of the bed letting the drum beat as the mantra echoed like a broken record, "Nope, he isn't dead."

I looked back at his still, cold body and I swore I saw his chest move. The denial was so real but the lie that I had been repeating in my head was shattered into a million tiny pieces when the police officer looked sadly at my brother and me and said, "I am sorry for your loss."

We were stunned. I started to worry about my brother because he and my dad had that *Sanford and Son* type bond. They argued nonstop ,but they loved one another in a way that could not be described. I wanted to be sure that my brother was okay, so I started making phone calls and focusing on how to best help him through the tragedy of finding our father dead.

Other than the tears that I shed in the moments immediately after seeing my dad's cold, lifeless body seated in his bed, I didn't cry for a long time. My time of crying was in his bedroom when I was sitting at his feet in denial that he was gone. I'd tried so hard to convince myself that he was still alive and that he was just sleeping hard after drinking a forty-ounce bottle of malt liquor. Besides, who had time to cry?

Let the Calls Begin

I had to start calling family and friends to tell them that my father had passed away. As I made the calls, an interesting pattern emerged. It seemed that every family member and every friend I notified said that they had either seen or spoken with my dad the day before. I recall thinking that my dad knew he was about to leave this earth. He would always ask my brother and me, "What will you do when I die?" Unnerved by his asking, I would always reply, "I don't want to talk about that!" or "Dad, you ain't going nowhere."

And yet, there we were -- dad had died.

As I called and told people of my father's passing, they responded to the news with any mixture of screaming, wailing, and silence. Most were just in shock. They could not believe he was gone.

I could not believe it either.

Before the funeral home picked up my dad's body, his house was like a wake. Neighbors came over and went upstairs to "view" dad's body.

I was there to comfort them. I had no time for crying. I had to be strong. My mom, who lives in Maryland, drove so quickly from her home to Philadelphia that someone would have guessed she lived a few miles away from my dad's home. Mom came in and shed so many tears over daddy. Seeing her that way only broke my heart again, but I remained strong.

I have since remarried; but as I made calls and consoled our weeping mother and the family and friends who filed through dad's home that day, my brother was out with my husband.

He intimately understood the pain of enduring the death of a loved one because his dad had died too. They were gone for hours. I was annoyed. There was work to do. All I could think about was the funeral arrangements.

Finally, my husband and brother returned to my dad's home. "Are you going to be okay staying here?" they asked me. "Yes, I'll be fine. I'm good." I wanted to spend the night at my dad's house. My husband told me that he would take care of our boys and assured me that he was fine. He also encouraged me by saying, "Take the time you need." My husband had spent time consoling my brother, but in addition to making funeral arrangements, I also wanted to make sure that my brother was okay.

That night, I remember laying in the same bed where my daddy died. Oddly, I couldn't cry. I believe that since, deep in my subconscious mind my dad was still alive, my tears just would not flow.

The Cleaning Brigade

In the tradition of every elder I know; my grandma and great aunts came to dad's house the day after he died. Like soldiers, they dispersed themselves and handled the tasks at a hand. These women were strong women who didn't cry at their own mothers' funerals, so I knew better than to cry around them. The buckets, brooms, dusting and all the soap and solution that make for a stellar cleanup crew was splishing and splashing through every room and on every level of my daddy's home. As a matter of fact, at one point, I felt like I was in the way. These ladies were on a mission to clean dad's home before the masses of card-carrying loved ones and their condolences came flooding through daddy's door with wholesale volumes of chicken, juice, cake and other popular funeral fare.

They were right, the house should not be dirty when company came. As the reality of dad's passing settled upon me, I felt like the weight of the world was on my shoulders. Nonetheless, I also felt that I needed to show the cleaning brigade where things were and that I needed to help them. I followed their orders and I did not cry. All the while, I wished and even looked for my dad to walk right through that door.

However, my wishing and looking toward the door for dad eventually stopped for good. Reality set in when I viewed his body. It was very hard to see him lying there. He looked like he was asleep. I didn't cry. I had to be strong.

Finally, on the day of my dad's funeral, I cried profusely. The denial had ended, and God's healing had begun.

So, during that service, as I stood in the church and looked at the young lady who had found her father dead, I looked into her eyes and told her that I had been where she was and that I knew how it felt to lose your dad. We hugged, and she thanked me. I didn't want to say anything to her that day. I didn't want to share my story with that young woman, but because of the

Holy Spirit prompting me, I shared. I was immediately glad that I did.

We all need to know, especially in times of difficulty, grief, and loss, that our sisters see us and that we are not alone.

We Wear the Mask

Sometimes the masks we wear make it impossible for us to give and receive the help and love that our sisters try to share. I know because I like to hide or, as they say in the streets, "I like to be in the cut." I am comfortable being in the background. I like that no one can see me. I'm like an owl. You do not know I am there unless I show myself. I am intelligent, I strive for perfection, and I do not like attention. To avoid competition, I work quietly, and I avoid confusion. However, if drama shows up at my door, I know exactly how to handle myself. Otherwise, you will never know my feelings, because I mask them so well.

As the brilliant Paul Laurence Dunbar penned:

We wear the mask that grins and lies,
It hides our cheeks and shades our eyes,
This debt we pay to human guile;
With torn and bleeding hearts we smile,
And mouth with myriad subtleties.

Why should the world be over-wise,
In counting all our tears and sighs?
Nay, let them only see us, while
    We wear the mask.

We smile, but, O great Christ, our cries
To thee from tortured souls arise.
We sing, but oh the clay is vile
Beneath our feet, and long the mile;
But let the world dream otherwise,
    We wear the mask!

In every friendship I had, I was the calm one. When my friends got emotional and excited, I could get emotional and excited too, but when it came to feelings, I just had the mindset that no one needed to know how I really felt. In almost every one of my relationships -- even when I felt the relationship was coming to end-- I held on to my friend because I didn't have the courage to say, "This isn't working for me any-more." How do you do that? I realized that I was invested in emotionally pleasing my friends although the relationships were often one-sided in terms of trying to do what was best for one another. In many instances, if they were alright, I would just pretend that I was alright too. I rarely admitted when I was hurting inside.

A perfect example is a friendship that a girlfriend of mine and I developed. She and I became close because our husbands were good friends. We were pregnant at the same time, hung out together, worked out together, and it just so happens that we even separated from our husbands at the same time. I won't say it was planned because our marital issues were very different. Nonetheless, we stayed in touch and hung out.

I remember that I wanted to transfer to the same department she worked in. I was so ex-cited about the opportunity. When I told her that I was applying for the job, she asked me why. She went on to explain that the depart-ment she worked in was horrible and that she would not recommend that I apply for the job. I could have assumed that she was just looking out for me, but as we continued to talk about what she called "issues" on the job, I realized that the "issues" were more about her personal likes and dislikes than about the job or about the opportunity that I'd have there. I mentioned to her that I handle issues differently than she and that I was still going to apply for the job. Her response was something along the lines of "good luck." Her blatant lack of encouragement about something that I was so excited about made me question whether she had my best interest at heart. She was supposed to be my good friend. Still, I never said anything to her about it. Instead I just remained silent and hurt. As time passed, our relationship faded. I wasn't mad that we were no longer close friends, but I do regret never telling her how I felt. I wonder if I had risked taking off my mask and opened up to her, if she would have better understood and supported me in a time when I really needed to be seen and to know that I was not alone.

Intergenerational Sisterhood Matters

For years, my girlfriend circle was always close to my age. I had a notion that women who were younger than I could not teach me anything and that women who were older than I couldn't relate to me. Thankfully, I have banished those false notions because time has taught me that we need sisters of all sorts in our circles.

During my time at one company, I became close to a woman who was the same age as my mother. After I divorced and started dating, I would share my stories about the men I dated and go into all the funny details. She and I had wonderful, refreshing conversations every Monday as we reflected on our weekends and I learned that she lived a rich, busy, sometimes complicated life--just like I did. I remember the first time my friend invited me to hang out with her crew. At first, I thought, "Nawh, ya'll will get tired and not want to party anymore, but I could not have been more wrong. I had the best time ever with my "old heads" as I affectionately called them. I started to wonder, "Why am I having more fun partying with my older

girlfriends than with women who are my age?"
It was all about perspective. For my mature sister-friends, getting together was about enjoying
life, celebrating each other, laughing, loving,
and living out loud. On the other hand, with too
many of my younger sister-friends, getting together was all about pretending and competing,
"Where do you work?", "What do you do?",
"Who do you know?", "What social organiza-
tions do you belong to?" That's too much
pressure. My old-head crew--they don't care
about those things one bit.

I hung out with everyone from bus drivers to attorneys. No one knew, and no one cared,
what profession anyone was because everyone
was most interested in enjoying life. I learned
how to deal with relationships with men. My
mature girlfriends would laugh and say, "Girl,
we don't chase nobody. We let them chase us!"
It was common for anyone of them to say,
"Come by my house to grab a bite to eat." If I
asked, "Why, are you having an event?" They'd
reply, "No, girl, because I am cooking. The girls
will be there, and you are invited too." My relationship with these women matured me and

gave me a different perspective on life. I learned that life is not about material things and status. Life is about the kind of person you become. Life is about enjoying yourself and the people you love. Life is about not being perfect and learning to be okay with that. Life is about saying to your sisters, "I see you and you are not alone."

I became friends with a young woman I met through her parents. We immediately clicked became friends good friends. Her immense love for and desire to help her friends moves and inspires me.

One year, we were doing the Daniel Fast to start the New Year. It was my first time participating in the fast and I immediately told her that it was going to be hard for me to give up coffee. "We will pray about that," she said. I went on to explain that I couldn't live without coffee and that I must have it every morning because if I did not, I would get caffeine withdrawal, headaches, and become irritable. Unphased by my mini panic attack over the mere thought of going without my coffee, she replied again, "We will pray on it." I felt like she wasn't hearing anything I was saying. I felt like yelling, "Girl! do you hear me?"

After the fast was over, I thanked her. I didn't get one headache and didn't miss not drinking the coffee either.

A couple of years later, we fasted together again. I told her that I wouldn't keep up with the fasting group on social media because I was "fasting" from social media. She asked me why? I told her that I needed to get offline to spend more time with God. She simply said, "You don't need to fast from social media, you just need to believe God for more discipline." That was a blunt, but true response. Again, I thanked her. She is such a blessing in my life.

I tried to hide my truest thoughts, feelings and opinions. I tried to wear the grinning mask, but both my younger and older girlfriends were used by God to get beyond my mask. I learned through these friendships, that no matter the age, no matter the culture, and no matter the socioeconomic background, we can all learn and benefit from one another. We all need our sisters. We all need to be seen and we all need to know that we are not alone.

SHARE

Chapter 2

It's Okay to Ask for Help

"Even when you make your own mess, you can still ask for help."

~Maxine L. Johnson

In addition to seeing our sisters and allowing ourselves to be seen, we must grow into being able to share and into discerning when to ask for help. We have to learn to share our wisdom, patience, information, love, time, pain, joy, successes, and failures without fearing judgement from our sisters and without judging our sisters, despite where they are in their process.

Interestingly, my dad, my cousin and a difficult life experience I had shaped my perspective on how important it is to know when to ask for help and on how important it is to know what information to share or whether to share at all.

Pride Can Block Progress

"You have to make do with what you've got," my dad would often say. It means that you have to make the best of what you have. Before I went to college, a neighbor gave me access to long-distance calling as a gift. I was so excited to receive long-distance service because it meant that I could keep in touch with my boyfriend who was back at home. I ran the bill up to seventy dollars in one month and had to pay for it so that our long-distance service wouldn't be interrupted. When I called home to ask for help with paying the bill, my dad asked me one question, "Did you call me seventy dollars' worth?" We both knew that I had not. As a matter of fact, I'd barely called home at all. Then my dad said to me, "You made your bed, now it's time to lie in it." That meant that I had made the situation what it was and that I would have to deal with the consequences. So, when I came home, I worked and was able to pay off the bill.

Although my dad was right to make me pay for my calls, sometimes I think that my father's decision to make me responsible for myself that day, is one of the reasons why I rarely ask for help when I should. There have been times in my life when I was tested to, what felt like, the point of no return. Even then, I'd hesitate to ask for help. I may have had to ask, but I never really wanted to ask. When we feel compelled to put on a mask and pretend as if all is well despite that our worlds are truly crumbling, we have to reject the pride that blocks us from getting the help we need. Asking for help can be particularly difficult when you are the person who people go to for help, encouragement, and inspiration.

Why was I ashamed? I maintained a facade that I had it all together, but in reality, I really didn't.

I did not ask for help because of my pride.

The pride that I refer to is not the good feeling that we should all have about who we are. I am speaking about the type of pride that stops you from getting what you or your family need because you care so much about what people will think or say. The pride that stopped me from asking for help was negative. Gerald Cowen, contributor to the Holman Illustrated Bible Dictionary, writes that the negative pride that I am describing is "the undue confidence in and attention to one's own skills, accomplishments, state, possessions, or position. It is also a rebellion against God because it attributes to self the honor and glory that God deserves alone."

It was not good that I so fiercely resisted asking for help because of undue confidence in my own skills. What is it about you that makes you not ask for help?

My challenge is that I believed that I was my own source. It follows that, since I saw myself as the source that was responsible to supply what my family and I needed, that I'd often ask myself, how can I ask for help? How can the "go to person" say they do not know how to figure it out?

There have been many situations in which I always had another plan. It was like a self-made algorithm in my mind. If yes, then go here. If no, then follow the arrows and go the other way. We like to have plans A through Z, but life just isn't really like that. Sure, we can and should plan but we must also acknowledge and accept when we just have to do what my daddy said and "make do with what you got." Daddy, in his wisdom, shared a vital life lesson with me. He said, "When your back is up against the wall--throw your pride out the window and ask for help."

Think about it. What can you share? We all have vital lessons to share that will help another sister to gain the insight and courage to ask for the help she needs to move forward.

A Light in the Darkness

I will never forget the time I had no electricity for over a month. The man I was dating was unemployed (which is another story) and I was holding it down. He and I stayed between my house and his mother's house because I didn't want anyone to know the dilemma that I was in. My oldest son was away at college, so he was fine, but I had to tell my youngest son that he had to stay with his dad. He really didn't want to, but I needed to make sure that he had the necessities and comforts of home and his father would provide that for him. My ex-husband offered to help me but I refused his help. "Why," I reasoned, "should he help me when another man was living with me?"

My aunt allowed me to store food in her refrigerator and, in her own way, she empathetically let me know that I did not need to be living that way. My aunt could have helped me financially too, but again, I was adamant that I did not have the right to ask for help since a man was living there with me.

I lived for over thirty days in the dark. That experience made me realize that my circumstance was not just a matter of the lights in my house being off. I was figuratively in a dark place. I'd allowed my undue confidence to get in the way of taking care of business.

Finally, in spite of my shame, I asked God for help. Once I surrendered, I returned home from work, walked into the house and noticed the microwave clock blinking. I asked my boyfriend if he'd taken care of the bill. He said that he had not. My electricity was restored and to this day, I still don't know how my lights were turned back on. Although I don't do not know who paid the bill, I know that God helped me.

Even when we make our own mess, we can still ask for help.

Sometimes we are so hard on ourselves. When we make a mistake, we feel like we are failures. When we trip up, we feel like we cannot get up. It can be embarrassing. Guilt can make you become reluctant to do anything else because of the way people will look at and think of you. No one at all is perfect. Learning this was a hard lesson for me. Guilt can be paralyzing because it makes us feel as if we don't deserve grace due to incidents that we got ourselves into. Let's use my situation as an example. I mean, how could you allow for your electricity to be cut off?", "Don't you have a job?" "Don't you have a man living with you?", The guilt was overwhelming and frankly when you are in a bad place, especially a bad place that you put yourself into, no one wants to be lectured and scolded.

As sisters who help sisters, we need to re-member not to lecture and scold. Furthermore, as sisters who need the help of other sisters, we need to accept where *we* are--even if we hate it--and we cannot be ashamed to ask for help.

Sometimes silence is the key to weathering a storm. When I reflect on those close to me, I think about one of my relatives who I greatly ad-mire. How she approached a dilemma in her life taught me a lot about sharing and asking for help.

She is well educated, has a great professional career, is family-orientated and has a philan-thropic spirit. Every time she and I talk, it inspires me to do more and to give more of my-self. She inspires me to leave this world empty and not to look back with regrets. She reminds me that there is no place for complacency and no room for mediocrity and she affirms that there is always more to learn and always more to do. She champions the mindset that holding back our gifts and talents is simply selfish. She has always been a great inspiration!

I vividly remember the day I found out that she'd lost her job. She had not said a word to me about being out of work. She never said, "I need help," so, when I found out that she was out of work, I wondered if I should reach out to see if she needed anything. We are related. I under-stand her and I knew that, as a rule, we don't ask for help because we make it our responsibility to figure it out. We'd talked often. There was no mention of her job status. She did not miss a beat. She landed a job that far exceeded how great we all thought her former job was.

Sometimes, not sharing our need is the right thing to do at certain times and phases in our process. Life goes on whether we ask for help or not. When one door closes, another door opens and, sometimes, the door to our place of comfort has to slam closed in order for another opportunity to open. My cousin understood all of those truths and she did not decide to share her struggle with me while she was in the middle of that storm. Timing is essential. Be wise. Sometimes, not asking for help in certain seasons, or from certain people, is the right things to do.

Living without electricity shone light on how toxic my relationships were. I was living in the dark, but through that difficult situation and through my sharing my hard time with others (although I would not allow them to help by giving me money), my eyes were opened. I was able to reflect on myself and to decide that neither God nor I wanted me to live that way.

Do not get used to living in the dark. It is a place of penalization, mediocrity, and complacency. Move out of the dark places and forge ahead with the courage to share your story, your needs, and your wisdom and with the courage to ask for help when asking is the right thing to do for you.

Wilma Rudolph said, "Never underestimate the power of dreams and the influence of the human spirit. We are all the same in this notion: The potential for greatness lives within each of us."

We know we can share and ask for help, but the courage and change come into our lives and into the lives of others when we can discern when to actually share and ask.

CARE

Chapter 3

We Can Help One Another

"You feel unstoppable when you know who you are. Especially when you have a band of sisters to help you become her."

~Maxine L. Johnson

All five components of creating global communities of change demand that we care about one another. When we see ourselves clearly and allow others to see us, to share with us in a variety of ways, and to care about what really matters, we create change and we help one another. A prerequisite to helping someone is to care about them. That's important.

It is as important for sisters to care more about themselves.

Let's Elevate Self-Care

After divorcing and navigating through several relationships, I had to finally stop and ask myself, "What are you trying to find?" Attention? Companionship? A boyfriend? Another husband? Ultimately, I realized that I didn't truly know myself.

I needed to focus on self-discovery and self-care. We tend to lose ourselves when our foundation is fractured. My foundation was shattered a number of times in my life, but especially when I lost my father, and when I divorced. At one point in my healing process, I'd decided to see a therapist. While working with that therapist, I began to ask myself so many questions. I wondered and challenge myself with questions like, "Why are you dealing with this?", and I asked myself, "What do you want for yourself? Who are you? What do you like and dislike? What do you enjoy doing?"

While I couldn't answer all of the questions right away, they were questions that I needed to explore and that I eventually did answer and the process started me on my path to wholeness through self-care. Sisters! We need to stop putting our needs last and start to make caring for ourselves, at least a fraction of the way we care for others, our top priority.

Getting to know yourself is a journey and, frankly, it can be a hell of a trip.

As we move forward with the goal of helping a sister by first helping ourselves, we have to remember not to get distracted with all of the sights and scenery on the journey, so that we can focusing on the getting ourselves and our sisters to our intended destinations.

Let's Fight for Self-Care

Even mold is useful. There is a purpose in nature for everything -- even nasty old mold. When mold rots, the food decomposes and returns to the soil, giving the soil the nutrients and vitamins that it needs to grow even more food. Similarly, when we go through healing and deliverance, our flesh rots. As the Spirit guides us, the unproductive desires, thoughts, and behaviors we have die. As a result, we get more of what we need to be healthy and whole enough to take care of ourselves and the people we love.

I am the mother of two boys. I have always believed that while I can't raise men on my own, I can teach my sons how to love and be responsible and I did that. Yet, the more self-reflection I did, the more I realized that the very best way for me to teach them about love and responsibility was to be more loving of myself. I invested time, effort, and money into finding my niche, passion, desire and dreams. I asked myself, "What example can you show your sons?" I knew that hating on their dad didn't help any of us so I never said a negative thing about their father and I am so glad that I didn't --they eventually found out on their own. Through it all, my sons and I learned to love ourselves, one another and the larger community around us unconditionally.

First marriages are not all bad. In everything, we must look for our lessons and we must not constantly rehash our losses. This means we choose to abandon ideas like:

- I will get you before you get me.

- I will strike first and be sure the sting is so hard that you can't strike back.

- I will not be hurt again.

After losing my dad and dealing with the divorce, I made a conscious decision to go back to school. Finally, I was going to care for others, but I was going to make it my priority to do me too.

Women today are faced with countless challenges and obstacles. We are faced with caring for our husband and the children and even the pets in our home. Sometimes we are compelled, or required, to take care of extended family and friends too. We truly experience, as the scriptures say, being all things to all men. In our homes we are everything from executives, to nurses and professional drivers. We simultaneously serve as psychologists, housekeepers, teachers, interior decorators, chefs, schedulers, event planners and best friends. When a man, child, or pet needs a hug, we are there. If they need medicine to take, we are there. I learned, from observing every person or thing in my care that when they are in need or want of something, they will ask me for it without hesitation. Yet, many women feel like they have lost the permission to ask for help.

When things get rough, we are the ones who get called upon. "Woman, do you have money? Woman, can you take me here?, Woman, can you pick me up? Woman . . .?" It is easy to see how we can feel so stretched and overwhelmed that we lose ourselves in the incessant pleasing and doing for others.

Developing a self-care mindset takes courage and can require us to drastically alter, and even leave, family relationships. This can include our relationships with our children. It took me a long time to let go because I had embraced the philosophy that I needed to make sure that my sons were alright even though they were no longer little boys. They'd become men who would one day become husbands and fathers. Would it be fair for me to stagnate their growth and emasculate them by treating these men like boys? I decided that I would not rob my little sisters--their future wives of good providers and protectors by babying my sons. That would be selfish, and I did not want to deny the women they'd come to study, work with and eventually marry from having a good man. I had to have the courage to cut the strings and allow them to be men, even when doing so meant watching them fall. I had to have the faith that they would be resilient enough to get up and try again.

I made a conscience choice to wo"man" up and to let go.

When I decided to return to school to finish my degree, my ex-husband asked me, "Who will watch our sons while you're at school?" I'd wrongly assumed that he would, but he swiftly made it apparent, that he had other plans.

Remember H.A.S. component number two? Yes, indeed. If I was going to even have a chance at helping others by first helping myself, it was time for me to share my new goals and aspirations with people who cared and ask for help. I was determined to make a change in my life and to elevate my self-care, but I needed help.

I'd already registered for school and my classes were paid in full, but there was no plan in place for child-care for my sons. Who would be there to feed them when they got home? Who would help them with their homework after school? Who would take them to football, basketball, and track practices, make sure they washed, and tuck them in at bedtime?

I found the courage to say, "I cannot do this on my own!" Instead of altogether sacrificing what I wanted and needed to do, I asked for help. I called my cousin and told her my plans for school. She was excited for me and asked me what I needed. I told her that I needed someone to be with my sons while I was in class. Instantly, she said, "No problem! I've got you." I was relieved.

As time passed and my sons became older, I decided to continue my education and go to graduate school. By then, they were old enough to stay home by themselves, but I needed to have someone take them back and forth to their athletic activities. My cousin who helped me while I completed my undergraduate degree was not available. It just did not make sense to have her come from another part of the city to take my sons to their athletic activities. So, in the interest of keeping myself on the list of people to care about, it was time for me to ask for help again.

My neighbor, who is like an aunt to me, lived a few doors away from my home. I asked her if she would be willing to take my sons to their practices while I was in class. Just as quickly as my cousin agreed to help me years earlier, my neighbor said she would help me get through this next phase of my journey. "Help you? No problem!", she said. As a matter of fact, she became so involved that she was a football and basketball auntie for every sport the boys played except for track. She was involved in every aspect of their youth sports activities. She said track and field was just too hot for her. It takes a sisterhood to raise our families and to care for ourselves.

I have learned through my experiences that you have to have the courage to ask for the help. Things just work out so much better for everyone when you do. Once you ask for help, your sister-girlfriends are happy to pitch I in. The more I made my needs known, the more I found out that I was not alone and the more my sister-girlfriend circle grew. The weight of keeping my sons' sports schedule by herself was no longer my aunt's alone. The sports' moms from every team banned together and created a schedule so we could rotate pick-ups and drop-offs. We all looked out for each other because we were all in it together. We wanted what was best, not just for our children, but for ourselves too. And we had grown to learn and appreciate the tremendous value of caring for our families, for one another, and for ourselves.

CHANGE

Chapter 4

Start with the Woman in the Mirror

"Look at the lessons not the losses; with every sacrifice there is a gain and with every gain there is a struggle."

~Maxine L. Johnson

As I have shared throughout the book, I was very close to my father. I enjoyed gleaning from his wisdom and knowledge about life and about me. He would tell me things about myself that I had never recognized or considered. When I think about it, he always encouraged me with his words and told me that I would excel at everything I did as long as I used my mind. My dad advised me not to get caught up in material things by teaching me how to make do with what we had, which made me resilient and gave me both the mindset and the skills needed to survive anything that comes my way. His manner with me made me strong but sensitive and eventually taught me the importance of caring for myself and others and of asking for help when necessary. He embodied the components of H.A.S. that we have covered so far and that is why he was loved by so many people. My dad saw me. He shared his successes, struggles, joy and pain. He also shared what he had to help others. Dad was not selfish. He cared for me and for others and taught me that it was as important for me to take care of myself.

My dad often told me the story of how I nearly died when I was younger. He explained that I was a survivor of bacterial meningitis, an illness that usually kills people within days, but I survived. My dad taught me how to be humble, but confident. He taught me that I did not need to compete with others and that I did not need titles, certain degrees, or the accolades of anyone. He made me believe that I was special, just because I was me.

I certainly saw myself through my dad's eyes. For so long, and in so many ways he was like a mirror to me. I could constantly check, see, and change my life as needed by looking to my dad.

One of the funniest stories I recall from my childhood was when my parents attended a cocktail party that was hosted by my mother's job. Mom worked at a prominent hospital in Philadelphia. Dad explained that before events at her job, my mother would always tell him to behave himself because there were many doctors and executives present at the events. She did not want to be embarrassed. "Be on your best behavior!" she'd fuss at him. At this one party that dad loved to talk about, he was asked what he did for a living. My dad was employed by a transportation company as a janitor. Under strict orders to be on his best behavior, when a man came up to him at the party and asked,

"What do you do for a living?" Dad looked at him and said, "I am a janitorial engineer and what do you do?" The man replied, "I am a manager at Genos!" Dad loved telling me that story to remind that I never have to change or alter who I am to fit in anywhere.

Change Takes Time

Self-reflection and assessment take time. We all go through stages in life and in each stage, we learn valuable lessons about ourselves and others. Like a butterfly, we undergo a metamorphosis of sorts too.

We go through different stages and phases with everything from hairstyles, to friends, to what we enjoy doing socially. I laugh at myself because I can say that I have had every hairstyle and color except blue, green, and yellow. The fact is that with each change of my look, I was still trying to figure out who I was. "What does Maxine like or want?" In so many phases, I could not answer that question. As odd as it may seem, each and every trial, tribulation, success or issue is an important part of becoming who you are supposed to be.

I enjoy talking to my mother and older women in my life who share their stories of how they overcame difficulties. Their stories are so compelling. "How did they do it?", I would think while listening, intrigued by their strength, as each woman, including my mom, explained how they approached and dealt with adversity. My mother prevailed through so much and I was right there to see her pick up all the broken pieces and start over again.

My mom is amazing! I think back to how my brother and I sat in classes at Temple University while she was completing her degree. We'd sit quietly, coloring and writing so that she could do what she had to do while my dad was at work. I remember finding my mom asleep at a track meet because she'd worked all night only to pick us up to take us to a meet that lasted all day long so that her only place to rest was at the track. In so many ways, my mother also served as a model for me. When I was off-track, I used her examples as a mirror in which I could check myself to see what changes I needed to make.

A Wonderful Change

Things started to change in my life rapidly and for good when I gave my life to Jesus Christ. The closer I got to Him, the more I learned about myself. One of the most important things I learned was that He loves me just the way I am. I didn't need to put on a front. I only needed to be me-- fun, silly, positive Maxine. Like a caterpillar who welcomed the change, I was getting ready for my wings.

In the butterfly's process, the chrysalis is where the metamorphosis occurs. The chrysalis is a holding space where transformations occur before the butterfly gets her wings. As sisters, we go through our own sort of chrysalis too. We go in one way and come out another. In the chrysalis, we don't worry about pleasing people, we focus on pleasing God. In the chrysalis, we learn that no matter what hairstyle we have, we are still beautiful. It is in the chrysalis is where we learn to say, "No." It is in the chrysalis where we find out who our true friends are.

The chrysalis is a life-changing phase of development. When the caterpillar emerges from the chrysalis, she uses her wings to break out of the cocoon. It is essential that she break out of the cocoon herself because in doing so her wings get strong and grow. Eventually, the butterfly emerges — gorgeous, unique, and ready to fly away.

When you can fly, you feel so free. God has elevated us to seek more and to experience more so that in all things we can grow in Him. One of my favorite songs of worship is *Fly* by Jason Upton. I love when he says, "Going up to new atmospheres, new places. God has given you the air so fly!" That is my testimony. I feel unstoppable now, because I know who I am. I go after my goals. I work to make my dreams come true. His new Maxine just goes and gets it! All the years of fighting and struggling through it all were a part of the preparation that made me strong so that I would be prepared to do what I needed and wanted to do. Now it's your turn, The sky is the limit. It's all yours to explore and conquer. Go on sister, and fly!

H.A.S. Networks Work

When you are ready to fly, you meet other sisters who are flying too. Speaking with my sisters is like iron sharpening iron because we all want to get better, grow stronger, and help each other. Elevation in our personal lives is a great thing because the higher we go, the more we know and learn about ourselves. Each destination is a place of self-exploration. What I've learned is that when I want to seek new heights, God always places a sister around me to show me the way to go. It's amazing to me because I know not every woman has that experience.

Too many women tend to hate on each other and think that getting ahead is a competition, but it is not. We have to change that way of thinking. Winning means women elevating women to live out their purposes and to fulfill their personal goals — all of these purposes and goals are necessary and different. Think about it, we live in a world with billions of people; I believe there is something important and unique for each of us to contribute. "I gave it my all and I gave it my best!" Mediocrity and complacency are from the devil. They come into our lives and paralyze us so that we cannot move forward. This is where our sisters come in. Sisters show up asking the questions that we need, but do not want to hear. Sisters ask, "Did you enroll for your fall classes?", "Were you able to finish that chapter you were writing for your book?", "Did you call the doctor?", "Did you leave that man alone yet?" "How can I help you get that done?"

Sisters keep each other accountable. It's not a competition. If you want to compete, there are running events, swim meets, bike races, and other activities you can register for to compete, but when it comes to sisters on a mission to make positive change in this world – we are all in this together.

I love to work out because it makes me feel good and keeps me healthy. Still, some days I just do not feel like it. Life so easily gets in the way of taking care of my temple. Life--I have a meeting early in the morning or I oversleep, or I just have too much to do to get to the gym. However, I am grateful for my accountability sister-friend who texts and asks, "Did you work out? Oh you missed a day? So, what's your plan to make it up? Can you take a long walk instead?", and she is right, because every move counts! Whether we are talking about exercise or the work that you are placed on the earth to accomplish, we can't be still, we all need an accountability partner to keep us on task, because if we can't do what was planned, we have to quickly adjust the plan and still do something because every single move forward counts. My sister is a perfect example of why we need sister networks and of why H.A.S. works!

So, let's review. At some point in your development, you need and have to change something about your thinking, your schedule, your relationships, or some aspect of your life. In order to know what to change and what not to change, as well as, when those changes should occur, you have to know yourself. It's hard to change when people's thoughts and opinions have such influence in your life, but if you are not changing, you are not growing and H.A.S. requires us all to both change and grow.

In my twenties, I found myself in full fledge family mode. I was a wife with two children. My college life was short lived, but completing my degree never left my mind. At that phase of my life though, my focus was on being a good mother and wife. Everything I did was centered around my family and nothing was focused on me. I felt sad that I'd lost my style and my confidence due to my focus on taking care of everyone else. That was my first priority. I did work out so that I could remain a decent size, but emotionally, I was not present. When I'd see my high school friends become college graduates, it hurt me to my core. I was so hard on myself about the sacrifice I'd made of family over my own education, but when you have a sister-friend who reminds you of your worth, it brings you peace. Thank God I had that friend.

During my first year of college, I found out that I was pregnant. The conversation of keeping the baby or getting an abortion came up. I toiled with the decision mentally and emotionally. It brought back memories of being a sixteen-year old, pregnant girl who had to complete one more year of high school. I was an honor roll student, scholar-athlete and school officer. Since I did not fit the stereotype, people would think, "How could she be pregnant?", but I was young and made the choice to have an abortion. Two years later, when I learned that I was expecting in college, although I was not emotionally and mentally as strong as I needed to be, I knew that I had to keep going. I was pregnant again. Still devastated by the decision I'd made at sixteen not to keep my child, I decided that I was going to keep my baby this time.

My friend from high school told her mom that I was pregnant. I didn't know what to expect from her mother, but frankly, I was upset with my friend because I was trying to deal with this myself. I did not need a conversation with her mother to add to my guilt and disappointment. When my friend's mom, Ms. Vivian, called me, she told me her story. Ms. Vivian was a mother to two children who she had at the ages of nineteen and twenty. Years after having her children, she finished her schooling and has a good job. Her point, "Before you make your decision whether to keep the baby or abort the baby, remember you have to live with that decision, not your family or your friends." Now, my focus was not on me but on my unborn child. So, I decided to endure the delay, have my baby, and keep moving forward.

By the time I was thirty, I was separated and contemplating whether I was going to get a divorce. The notion of going back to school was eminent but how would I do so with a full-time job and still keep the boys active in sports? I did not want them to suffer because of my goals and I was determined to finish my degree. As I shared with you, I asked for help and everything worked out for the good of my boys, my cousin who helped me, the sister-group we formed back then, and for me.

By that time in my life I had changed. While I carried the important lessons that they'd both taught me in my heart and head forever, I was no longer looking through the eyes of my dad or my mom to figure out who I was. I knew more about myself, what I wanted, and what I desired for myself. Now, I was looking at the woman in the mirror and making her responsible to change her ways and doing so did nothing but make me stronger.

In my early forties, three years later, I thought, I should have been much farther along, but I know now, that the mirror had to be cleaned in order for me to see everything about myself that I needed to see so that I could move towards my destiny, and it is still a journey. It was not someone else's walk. It was mine. I realized I couldn't compare myself to others and that I couldn't think about what others thought about me. Besides, my mother used to tell me, "You never listened to me, so why are you listening to people you don't even really know!" She had a great point.

When I look in the mirror now, I don't see the scar tissue that was left from every trial, I don't see the wounds of a broken heart and I no longer carry the guilt of my choice to terminate a pregnancy.

I am who I am by the grace of God.

Life isn't easy and in retrospect I'm glad it wasn't easy because it allowed me to ask myself the hard questions such as: "Do you deserve being treated this way? Don't you want more for yourself? What are your goals? What are your dreams?" Life for me was not easy, but I don't have regrets. When I decided to return to college, I talked it over with my mom and all she said is, "You can do it!" I have never denied myself an opportunity because it was not going to be easy.

I look at life like a triathlon. I have participated in a triathlon. There are three parts: swimming, biking, and running. The run came easy to me because I have been a runner since I was nine years old. The challenge for me, was swimming. "Why would I enter into a race when I don't even know how to do everything required of me to participate?" I was not worried at all. I knew that I just needed to be trained. Interestingly, I *thought* I knew how to swim until I was invited to swim laps with some friends. When I observed how easily they swam laps, I realized very quickly that I really did not know how to swim. I knew how to doggie paddle.

Learning to swim as an adult was both challenging and humbling. I had to learn the strokes, how to breathe, and build up stamina. It was hard. On top of learning how to swim, I had to train to run and bike. Riding in this race is not like a casual ride in the park, it's riding as if in an endurance race. It was hard. In between each discipline is what is called transitions. The run is first, then there is transition one. After the swim, I felt like I could accomplish anything, but then there was the bike--transition two. I felt like giving up because my legs hurt, it was hot, and I was thirsty. Still, I had to run. My legs felt like bricks, but I had come too close to the end of that race to give up, so I didn't.

In so many ways, my life has been like a triathlon. At times I thought I knew how to do things that I did not know how to do, I learned lessons the hard way, I relied on help at some phases and rejected it at others, I felt amazing at some phases and stages and wanted to totally give up at others, but I knew that I'd come too far to give up and I knew that God didn't bring me as far as He had to give up on me — so I kept on pressing.

Thank God that I persisted, and continue to persist, through my change process. My doing so has birthed and developed this global H.A.S. sisterhood that together, we will keep nurturing Helping a Sister. will save, bless, education, instruct and help sisters all over the world to evolve not the powerful changes agents God designed them to be.

Throughout my life, I refused to reflect on the losses and instead looked for the lessons in it all. Even when I was sad or disappointed, I knew that with every sacrifice, there is gain and that with every gain, there is struggle. As I walked through the stages of my life, I could have easily decided to live in regret. I could have taken a seat at the table, blown up balloons and had a pity party, but what good would that have done?

There was no need for a pity party. The only thing I needed to do was change.

I have story upon story that would give me legitimate reasons to give up. Instead, I learned, I changed, and I kept moving forward. That is what H.A.S. is about. The movie reels of my life include a number of stressful times in which my decision to apply or benefit from another sister's application of the five H.A.S. principals rescued me.

I remember when the water where I lived was shut off. I had to wait until I got paid to restore it, but there were sisters who I knew and who helped me out. My aunt and friend lived several doors away from me at the time. They offered to help by supplying us water. I had five-gallon water jugs that my sons and I would fill up at my friend's home. She would say to us, "Don't go out the front door. Go through the back door. Everyone doesn't need to know your business." Thank God for her words of wisdom, because by that time in my struggle, I was tired and frankly didn't care. I had to keep moving, just like we handle the transitions in a triathlon.

We can't just sit in the transition spaces during the race. Likewise, we have to move on to the next phase in our lives.

I have both had cars repossessed and learned how to work the system to pay at strategic times to avoid the repossessions. Even when I received the knock at my door to notify me that I was being evicted in 30 days because the house had been foreclosed upon, I was numb, but so grateful that I had spoken with a sister-friend at work who connected me with a mortgage broker. I told her I didn't have money, but she said they would work it out. I told her my credit was bad. She said, "We will work it out," and she did.

I was approved for a mortgage to buy from the bank. We negotiated. They accepted. I became a homeowner. When it was time to go to settlement, I was told that I needed five-thousand dollars to close. I was devastated. I had no money. Although I knew of God, at that time in my life, I did not have a relationship with Him. Nonetheless, I did as my grandmom would say to do--I prayed. The mortgage broker called me and said, "I am so sorry. I made a mistake. You don't owe five-thousand dollars. You owe one-thousand dollars." God is awesome!

Living a life of mediocrity and accepting car repossession and utility shut offs as normal is not how God wanted me to live. I don't regret the things that I endured because going through those hardships taught me the importance of becoming a good steward of my finances. Every success and every failure taught me how to process the lessons and how to change.

Now, my trials are over and they serve as valuable lessons that I can share with my sons. Like the great Langston Hughes I can confidently tell them:

Well, son, I'll tell you:
Life for me ain't been no crystal stair.
It's had tacks in it,
And splinters,
And boards torn up,
And places with no carpet on the floor —
Bare.
But all the time

I'se been a-climbin' on,
And reachin' landin's,
And turnin' corners,
And sometimes goin' in the dark
Where there ain't been no light.
So, boy, don't you turn back.
Don't you set down on the steps.
'Cause you finds it's kinder hard.
Don't you fall now —
For I'se still goin', honey,
I'se still climbin',
And life for me ain't been no crystal stair.

MAXINE L. JOHNSON

CREATE

Chapter 5

A Global Band of Sisterhood: Iron Sharpens Iron

"One woman at a time, this Global H.A.S. movement is literally changing the world."

~ Maxine L. Johnson

Seeing, sharing, caring, and changing our lives and the lives of sisters across the globe the H.A.S. way inevitably creates a movement, a band, a sisterhood who operates as global change agents for women everywhere.

I have endured and overcome a lot of in my life, but I didn't have to go through all of it alone. I am grateful for sisters and friends who said, at every stage and phase, "I've got your back." "I can help you. What do you need?" My lessons became their lessons. My trials became an example for my sisters of what not to do. Our allegiance became a powerful force that roared, "Together, we can and will get through this," and every single time — we did. We got through it! In the process, the lessons that I shared with you through my stories were born of the experiences I lived through.

Yes, I have ministered broadly and helped women near and far using the techniques and skills and strategies that I know. However, what is most compelling, is not that I have observed that seeing, sharing, caring, changing and creating in communities of women transforms lives. What is most compelling is that I know that the five core components of the movement can help sisters everywhere, because the principles never failed to help me.

Create Global Communities of Change

Proverbs 27:17 says, "Iron sharpens iron, so one person sharpens another." How can we sharpen each other as sisters? We can strategically create

H.A.S. communities that become safe havens for women everywhere.

First, we have to SEE our sisters and ourselves as God sees us. We have to look at *and* see one another, both as we are, and as we will become, remembering that we all grow in different phases and stages, yet all by God's great grace.

Second, we have to expand and embrace the various ways in which to SHARE as we go through trials in our lives. We have to remember that even when we make our own messes, God does not hate us. We are still eligible to ask for help — and we should.

Thirdly, of the countless ways in which we as women CARE for others, we must make it our utmost priority to care for ourselves too. As we strengthen, encourage, beautify, and uplift ourselves, we create a source that is sustainable and pure from which to do the same for our husbands, daughters, son, mothers, fathers, brothers, extended families and communities at large.

Fourth, CHANGE must start with the woman in the mirror. Yes, that means you. We need to decide what to change about ourselves and about our lives and what not to change. We need the help of God to discern what to keep and what to remove and when.

When we embrace and apply all of these concepts, we inevitably CREATE Global Communities of Change.

If within these communities you take the courage to reach out and share your story with your sisters, you will help someone else. It's not easy to share our stories, because we are never sure who would use our story or how, and we do not know how our truths will cause us to be judged and perceived. Still, sharing your story is more important than anything that would stop you from sharing because, when told to the right sisters, at the right time, in the right way, only your story can rescue your sister from her despair. Creating Global Communities of Change includes these five H.A.S. promises to:

- Be supportive

- Be loving

- Be compassionate

- Be a listening ear

- Be a shoulder she can cry on

H.A.S. is not a program or an organization. H.A.S. is a mindset. It's a philosophy. It is a way of life. It is a movement. Adopt those you encounter as your sisters and remember that you don't have to be a mentor only. You just have to be a real, transparent, genuine sister. Regardless of the age or stage of life your sisters are in, you can glean and give--the relationship is reciprocal. It's not one-sided. We are open and we learn from each other. We also hold one other accountable because we have an opportunity and a responsibility to sharpen one another. Iron sharpens iron. This H.A.S. sisterhood is changing the worlds of sisters all over the globe.

Remember what Wilma Rudolph said, "Never underestimate the power of dreams and the influence of the human spirit. We are all the same in this notion. The potential for greatness lives within each of us."

We face many challenges and obstacles and many of our choices will affect us for the rest of our lives. However, today you made a great choice--the choice to become a better woman and to help other sisters, to become better women too.

Iron sharpens iron, so one sister sharpens her sister.

Manifest your greatness, dear Sister, because greatness does and H.A.S. always lived inside of you!

HELPING A SISTER

About the Author

Maxine L. Johnson is an ordained Itinerant Elder in the African Methodist Episcopal Church where she currently serves as the Pastor of Metropolitan AME Church in Lansdowne, Pennsylvania.

Recognized as a powerful preacher, God uses Maxine to share His message in a manner that is relevant, raw, and real. Her mission is to encourage, restore, and empower the people in our communities so that they can experience healing and wholeness. She focuses on sharing Jesus' power--His saving, healing, restoration, and reviving power--and His love.

A native of Philadelphia, Pennsylvania, Maxine received her Bachelor of Science in Human Resource Management and her Master of Business Administration from Rosemont College. She earned a Master of Divinity at Payne

Theological Seminary and is a graduate of the Samuel Elijah Prophetic College.

She is also an active member of Alpha Kappa Alpha Sorority, Inc.

Reverend Johnson is married to Joseph Johnson, Sr. and they are the parents of five children.

"When you fly, you feel so free. Sisters, take your wings, help a sister get hers, and let's soar!"

~ Maxine L. Johnson

Made in the USA
Middletown, DE
06 April 2019